LOST LINES OF WALES
CHESTER TO HOLYHEAD

TOM FERRIS

GRAFFEG

CONTENTS

FOREWORD

The aim of this series is to revive nostalgic memories of some of the more interesting and scenic railways which served Wales and visitors to the country when the railway network was in its prime.

In the case of the line covered in this volume, it also served many passengers both entering and leaving the country via that long established gateway to Ireland, the port of Holyhead. It was the route of the Irish mails and of the world's first named train called appropriately, the *Irish Mail*. Whilst much has changed since it first opened in 1848 that it continues to fulfil that original function of providing a vital link between the two islands, albeit from a railway point of view, in a reduced capacity, is a tribute to those who planned and built it all those years ago.

The line from Chester to Holyhead is not lost in the sense that some of the other long closed railways covered in this series are lost. There is a good service from Chester along the north Wales coast to Holyhead. There are even still some through trains from Holyhead to London Euston and two of the branches which fed traffic onto its tracks, those from Llandudno Junction to Llandudno and Bleanau Festiniog, are still open. What the line has lost is much of the infrastructure it had in its heyday, with many stations and signal boxes closed and four track sections reduced to two. This book will aim to recapture something of the atmosphere of that busy, traditional, steam-powered railway which was to be seen in years gone by.

The direction of travel on railway lines was usually described as being either Up or Down. On lines heading for London, such as this one, travel towards the capital was always in the Up direction and that away from London was described as being in the Down direction. On this line, that created an anomaly at Chester station where two expresses bound for London, both Up trains, could be seen leaving the station in opposite directions.

INTRODUCTION

The railway from Chester to Holyhead has always had two distinctive characteristics. On the one hand it has served the communities along its route for well over 150 years, linking the north coast of Wales to the rest of the country and in particular opening up the coast and its stunning hinterland of Snowdonia to tourism. Its other function was as a link between Britain and Ireland and its origins are to a large extent linked to the long and often turbulent relationship between these two islands lying off the fringe of western Europe. There was for centuries an imperative to get mail, information, people, occasionally even troops, across the Irish Sea as quickly as possible. The departure point of preference for mails destined for Dublin, for most of the last 500 years, has been Holyhead on the island of Anglesey/Ynys Mon, in north Wales. To be absolutely precise, Holyhead is actually located on another island called Holy Island, separated from Anglesey by a winding narrow channel and not on the main island itself.

In 1575 the journey on horseback from London to Holyhead took around 29 hours in summer and 41 in winter. Slow as this was, it was better than coaches could manage 200 years later. The need to improve communications between London and Dublin took on more urgency after the Irish Parliament was abolished by the Act of Union of 1800 which formed the United Kingdom of Great Britain and Ireland. The service gradually improved. In May 1820, steam ships replaced sailing vessels on the sea crossing and the opening of Thomas Telford's suspension bridge over the Menai Straits in 1826 connected Anglesey to the mainland for the first time. Even with this, in 1826, the average time it took to get mails from London to Dublin was about 50 hours. Matters improved in the 1830s with the opening of more stretches of Telford's great Holyhead Road which ran from Marble Arch in London to the quayside at Holyhead. In 1832 the journey north was scheduled to take 30 hours and 28 in the other direction. When the Holyhead Road was finally fully opened in 1836, the journey time for a mail coach was reduced but still took over a day to make the journey from London to Holyhead.

Ironically, in 1839, just a few years after Telford's great project was completed, the previously unheard of speed offered by the new railways led to the Irish mails being transferred from Holyhead to Liverpool, which from 1837 had a rail connection to London. Using the railway and steam ships from Liverpool meant that the mails could now reach Dublin in 22 hours if all went according to plan. Whilst this was quicker than Telford's road, the disadvantage of using Liverpool rather than Holyhead was the much longer sea journey.

The obvious solution was to build a railway to Holyhead if that was to be the railhead for the Irish mails. This was by no means assured, as several schemes focused on railways to Porth Dinllaen on the Llyn Peninsula as an alternative port to Holyhead before the north Wales coast route prevailed. The Grand Junction Railway opened a line from Crewe to Chester in 1840, linking it to Birmingham and London. The

next step came in July 1844, when the Chester & Holyhead Railway Act was approved by Parliament. This authorised the company to raise over £2 million to build its 85 mile long double track main line.

The engineer appointed to oversee this great undertaking was Robert Stephenson. The son of George Stephenson, who has been described as the father of the railways for his work on the pioneering Stockton & Darlington Railway which opened in 1825, Stephenson was faced with many challenges, including tunnels, sea defences and not least the building of a bridge over the Menai Straits. The first sod was ceremonially cut at Conwy in March 1845 and within a year over 5,000 navvies, many of them Irish, were employed building the line. The arrival of the navvies led to a number of serious disturbances between them and the locals in north Wales at this time. By August 1846 this number had increased to 12,000, many living in shanty towns that sprung up along the line.

Even before the line was fully open, a disaster befell it when on the 24th May 1847 the bridge carrying the line over the River Dee just outside Chester station collapsed as a train was crossing, killing five people. The subsequent enquiry blamed Stephenson's design, which used potentially brittle cast iron beams for the bridge's collapse under the weight of the train. Despite this setback to his professional reputation, he continued to work on the design for a revolutionary new type of bridge to carry the line over the Menai Straits. This was Stephenson's tubular bridge which was first tested at Conwy. Trains ran through wrought iron tubes which were fabricated on the shore of the Conwy Estuary and then floated into position on pontoons before being raised by hydraulic jacks.

The tubular bridge over the Menai Straits was a much greater challenge than the one at Conwy. The Admiralty had demanded that there was to be a 100ft clearance between the bridge and the water to allow high masted sailing vessels to pass under it. The top of the central tower of the Britannia Bridge, as it came to be known, was over 200 feet above the water. The two tubes which would carry the tracks were over 1,500 feet in length and were each fabricated from four sections. The first of these was floated into position in June 1849, but it was to be another year before the complex operation of raising the tubes into place was competed.

The 60 miles of railway from Chester to Bangor opened for passenger traffic on 1st May 1848, with four trains running on weekdays and two on Sundays, serving nine stations along the route. While work was going ahead on the section from Chester to Bangor, two locomotives had been shipped to Holyhead to assist with the construction of the line 20 miles across Anglesey, which opened for passengers from a temporary station at Holyhead to Llanfair P G, the station closest to the Straits, on 1st August 1848. Passengers were taken by coach across Telford's road bridge until the new railway bridge was completed. The first through passenger train to run the whole 264 miles from Holyhead to Euston was the 2.30pm express from Holyhead on 18th March 1850.

The costs of building the line had been much more than the C&H had bargained for and from the outset train services were worked by the London & North Western Railway, who bought the line outright in 1859. The mail steamers themselves had previously been operated by the Admiralty, but in 1850 the contract was put out to tender and awarded to the City of Dublin Steam Packet Company, much to the disgust of the Chester & Holyhead and their allies at Euston, who expected to get it after going to the trouble of building their new railway. With the mail contract came the prestigious initials RMS, standing for Royal Mail Ship, which preceded the names of the vessels themselves. The CoDSPC managed to hang on to the contract for most of the next 70 years.

The day the line across Anglesey opened, 1st August 1848, also saw the first running of the *Irish Mail*, the first named train in the world and the precursor of all those other prestigious trains which followed in its wake, the *Orient Express*, the *Brighton* Belle, the *City of New Orleans* and the rest of them. On that day the train left Euston at 8.45am and was due at Bangor at 5.25pm that afternoon. The mails were then conveyed by road to Llanfair on Anglesey and on by rail to Holyhead, arriving at the port at 6.45pm.

The history of this famous train tells us much about the line and how railways developed over the years. Line side apparatus to allow mailbags to be picked up and dropped off by a speeding train were used on the *Irish Mail* from 1854. The world's first water troughs were opened at Mochdre, between Conwy and Bangor, in 1860, allowing the engine to pick up water without stopping as it sped along. Sleeping cars were introduced in 1875 and restaurant cars in 1895. From 1st April 1897, Third Class passengers were permitted to travel on a train hitherto the preserve of First and Second Class only and the service was speeded up over the years. A new contract in 1860 stipulated that the run from London to Holyhead was to be accomplished in 6 hours 40 minutes. Only 35 minutes was allowed for the transfer of the mail to the steamer, which was given 3 hours 45 minutes to complete the sea journey. A penalty was imposed for every minute longer the whole journey took. By 1885 the journey time from London to Dublin had been reduced to 10 hours 20 minutes and by 1939 this was down to 9 hours and a quarter.

There were also two serious crashes involving the train in the course of the long history of the *Irish Mail*. The first of these occurred on 20th August 1868. On that day, the express passed Abergele at around 12.39pm, running under clear signals at about 40 mph, five minutes or so behind schedule. Ahead of it at the next station, Llanddulas, a goods train was being shunted out of the way to clear the Down line for the express. However, this was done in a singularly inept fashion. A rough contact between two sets of wagons sent those standing on the main line running away on the line on which the *Irish Mail* was approaching. There was no one in the brake van at the rear of the wagons to reapply the hand brake, which had been loosened by the impact and the wagons ran back down the line gathering speed. The curves and cuttings on this stretch of track meant that the driver of the express did not see them until they were only about 200 yards away. The impact derailed the engine of the express, but the heavy loss of life resulting from the accident was caused when wooden barrels in two of the wagons, holding about 1,700 gallons of paraffin, were ignited and turned the first four carriages into a funeral pyre for the unfortunate passengers travelling in them. In all 33 people died in what was the worst accident on Britain's railways up to that time. There were some similarities between the disaster of 1868 and another crash which occurred at Penmaenmawr in August 1950; six people perished in an incident which again involved a goods train and an express.

One final footnote to the history of the *Irish Mail* goes back to the dawn of the railway age and beyond. For over a century, at Euston station in London, a Post Office messenger would hand over a leather case containing a watch, set exactly to the correct Greenwich Mean Time at Greenwich observatory that day, to the Guard of the *Irish Mail*. Upon arrival at Holyhead, the watch was shown to an officer on the Kingstown boat which then carried the correct time on to Dublin. The watch was then returned on an Up service. This practice continued until 1939, with the *Irish Mail* bringing the correct time up to north Wales and across the Irish Sea. This was the succession to a similar procedure dating back to the days of the mail coaches, and shows how the railways played their part in uniting the kingdom, bringing accuracy and modernity to something as basic as having all parts of the country keeping to the same time. The name of the train no longer appears in the timetable and most mail has long since left the railways of Britain to clog up its roads, but there is today still a limited through service from Euston to Holyhead, a diminished but tangible reminder of this once famous train.

The London & North Western Railway which had operated the line since it opened became part of the London Midland & Scottish Railway when Britain's railways were amalgamated into four large groups in 1923, and in turn the line passed in 1948 to the newly-formed, publicly-owned British Railways. It still carried high volumes of traffic, including much of the freight for the steamers to Ireland and, in the other direction, trains bringing Irish cattle to markets in Britain. Many of the towns along the coast such as Rhyl, Prestatyn and Llandudno developed as tourist resorts with the coming of the railway and, after the Second World War, the opening of holiday camps also brought many holidaymakers to the line. The inexorable rise of car ownership, especially from the 1960s onwards, and improvements to the A55 road meant that a lot of this traffic was lost to the railways. Inevitably there were cutbacks. Track was rationalised and even though container trains were run to a new terminal built at Holyhead, in time much freight traffic was also lost to the roads. Steam had largely been replaced with diesel locomotives and multiple units by the mid-1960s, but the service frequencies if anything improved and relatively few stations were closed along the populous coastal strip served by the line.

Then, on the evening of 23rd May 1970, disaster struck. Some teenage boys, by their account on their way back from a party which had been cancelled, decided to explore the Britannia Bridge. One of them lit a page from a book he found on the track and dropped it between the girders. The fire quickly spread to the tar-coated wooden roofs of the tubes, the wind turning them into flues. The inaccessibility of the structure, poor water pressure and the absence of any fire hydrants near the bridge meant that despite the efforts of firefighters from both sides of

the Straits the inferno raged for nine hours, destroying the tubes but thankfully not the pillars which supported them. The line beyond Bangor remained closed for 18 months while the bridge was rebuilt.

There are more passenger trains on the north Wales coast line today than ever before. As well as trains to Chester, Manchester and Euston some services also run through to Cardiff and Birmingham. It remains a great scenic rail journey, hugging the coast for much of the way, and it is still providing an essential link both for those living in north Wales and for travellers to Ireland, as it has done since it opened all those years ago.

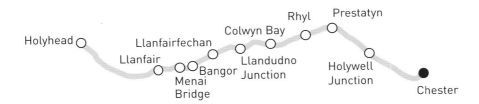

CHESTER

Holyhead ○　　　　Llanfairfechan ○　Colwyn Bay ○　Rhyl ○　Prestatyn ○
　　　　　　　Llanfair ○　　　　　　Llandudno ○　　　　Holywell ○
　　　　　　　　○○○ Bangor　Junction　　　　Junction
　　　　　　　Menai　　　　　　　　　　　　　　　　　● Chester
　　　　　　　Bridge

The starting point for our journey along the North Wales Coast line is Chester station, which at the time this view was taken in the 1950s would still have been called Chester General to distinguish it from the town's other station Chester Norgate, which closed in 1969. Opened in 1848, the station was used from that time by trains to and from the north Wales line and Crewe. It was also used by services from Shrewsbury and later by Great Western through expresses from Paddington to Birkenhead. The Chester

& Holyhead line had been worked from the outset by the London & North Western Railway, which became part of the London, Midland & Scottish group in 1923. Gradually, LNWR locomotives were supplanted by new LMS designs which continued to be used throughout the BR steam era. One class which regularly performed on north Wales services from the 1920s into the 1960s was the LMS Royal Scots. First introduced in 1927, they were extensively rebuilt from the mid 1940s onwards. Most of these locomotives

were named after regiments in the British Army. Here No 46119 *Lancashire Fusilier* pauses at the station on a Holyhead train. The small oval plate on the smokebox door is a shed plate indicating where the loco was based. At that time No 46119 was allocated to 7C, the code for Holyhead engine shed.

A long Holyhead goods train trundles
along one of the through roads at the
cavernous Chester General station
in October 1956, hauled by ex-LMS
class 5 4-6-0 No 45058. She was one
of the first members of this numerous
class to enter service, in December
1934, and was not withdrawn by BR
until March 1967. One peculiarity of
this station was that it was possible
to board expresses for London that
left the station in different directions.
Trains for London Euston headed east
via Crewe whereas those using the
former GWR line to London Paddington
via Shrewsbury headed west, sharing
the tracks to Saltney Junction with
trains bound for Bangor and Holyhead.

Shortly after leaving the station, the line to Holyhead breaches Chester's ancient walls, something that would not be tolerated today, and crosses the River Dee. The collapse of the original bridge on 24th May 1847, taking with it a train to Ruabon and killing five people, was a severe embarrassment for Robert Stephenson, the C&H engineer. The subsequent investigation into the disaster by the Board of Trade placed the blame squarely on his design for the bridge. A second span was later built beside the original double track formation as traffic increased, though only two tracks are in use today. To the right of the picture is Chester Racecourse, known as the Roodee. This compact track close to the city centre is the oldest racecourse still in use in England, records tracing it back to the sixteenth century. This view taken on 20th August 1951 is a reminder of the Great Western connection to Chester. A Manchester to Bangor passenger train, hauled by ex-LMS class 5 4-6-0 No 45410, is overtaking ex-GWR Grange class 4-6-0 No 6831 *Bearley Grange* on a mineral train which will take the line to Shrewsbury that diverges from the north Wales coast line at Saltney Junction, a mile or so to the south of the bridge.

On 27th June 1957, ex-LMSR class 5 4-6-0 No 45235 is seen near Saltney Junction with a westbound stopping train. Before nationalisation GWR trains had exercised running powers over this part of the route to reach their own line to Wrexham and Shrewsbury.

The locomotive hauling this train is a member of one of the most numerous classes of steam locomotives ever built in Britain. Designed by William Stanier, later Sir William, for the LMS in 1934, a total of 842 were introduced between then and 1951. Nicknamed Black Fives,

they were versatile and powerful locos which could be entrusted with almost any passenger or goods train and were found over the entire length of the vast former LMS system, from the far north of Scotland to west Wales and Dorset.

The four tracks were carried on westwards past Mold Junction, where the line to Mold and Denbigh diverged. Between there and the next station of Sandycroft on 10th July 1953, the former LMS Royal Train was recorded. The locomotive in charge and bearing the unique headlamp code reserved for such workings, three lamps along the buffer beam and one at the top of the smokebox, was Royal Scot class No 46151 *The Royal Horse Guardsman*. As was invariably the case with those locomotives designated to haul the Royal Train, it has been polished up to the highest degree. Built in 1930 and completely rebuilt in 1948 to the form seen here, No 46151 was withdrawn in 1963.

HOLYWELL JUNCTION

The main line ran alongside the estuary of the River Dee, straight and flat through Shotton and Flint until it came to Holywell Junction 17 miles from Chester. This was the junction for the Holywell branch, a very late addition to the railway map of north Wales, opened by the LNWR in 1912. The branch was built on the formation of a much earlier mineral line which had fallen out of use by the 1870s. Less than two miles long and very steeply graded, scheduled passenger and goods services ended in 1954 and it was officially completely closed in 1957. The branch was usually worked by push pull or Auto trains, with the locomotive at the rear. This was a system designed to save time at termini such as Holywell Town as the loco did not have to run round its train before the return journey to the junction. On the way up to Hollywell,

Holyhead ○ · Llanfairfechan ○ · Llanfair ○ · Menai Bridge ○○ Bangor · Llandudno Junction ○ · Colwyn Bay ○ · Rhyl ○ · Prestatyn ○ · Holywell Junction ● · Chester ○

the driver was in a compartment at the front of the coach which had controls linked to the engine, where the fireman remained, and they were reunited in the loco cab on the way back to the junction.

The terminus at Holywell was squeezed into a very compact site. LNWR and LMS Auto trains of different eras are seen in the two pictures. On 27th May 1947 ex-LNWR Webb designed auto-fitted 0-6-2T No 27585, a type first introduced in 1882, waits to leave Holywell Town with the 5.45pm service to Holywell Junction. The picture on the page opposite shows an ex-LMS version of the same method of operation, with auto-fitted class 2 2-6-2T No 41276, a type introduced in 1946, seen at the terminus. The door leading to the driver's compartment at the end of the coach is open.

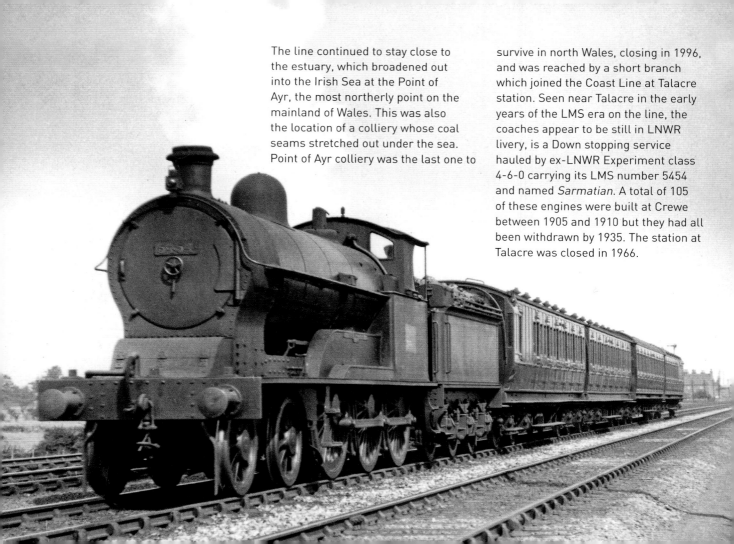

The line continued to stay close to the estuary, which broadened out into the Irish Sea at the Point of Ayr, the most northerly point on the mainland of Wales. This was also the location of a colliery whose coal seams stretched out under the sea. Point of Ayr colliery was the last one to survive in north Wales, closing in 1996, and was reached by a short branch which joined the Coast Line at Talacre station. Seen near Talacre in the early years of the LMS era on the line, the coaches appear to be still in LNWR livery, is a Down stopping service hauled by ex-LNWR Experiment class 4-6-0 carrying its LMS number 5454 and named *Sarmatian*. A total of 105 of these engines were built at Crewe between 1905 and 1910 but they had all been withdrawn by 1935. The station at Talacre was closed in 1966.

Three miles west of Talacre, the line reached the first of the big holiday destinations it had helped to create, Prestatyn. From a population of less than 1,000 in the 1840s, it grew rapidly and today has close to 20,000 inhabitants. Marketed as 'sunny Prestatyn' it had the almost obligatory holiday camp and its beaches have attracted legions of holiday makers over the years. On 23rd May 1936, LMS 2-6-0 No 2841 is seen at Prestatyn station. This was one of a class of 245 locos first introduced in 1926. They were nicknamed 'Crabs' because of the steep inclination of their cylinders, which gave them a slightly ungainly appearance.

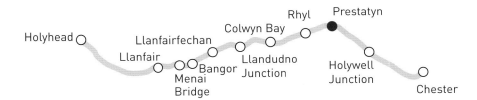

Holyhead Llanfairfechan Colwyn Bay Rhyl Prestatyn
Llanfair Bangor Llandudno Junction Holywell Junction Chester
Menai Bridge

Seen passing through Prestatyn station on 14th May 1936, is a long goods train hauled by Jubilee class 4-6-0 No 5685 *Barfleur*. Designed by Stanier for the LMS, 191 of these locos were built for express passenger duties in the 1930s. The class took its name from No 5552, which was named *Silver Jubilee* to mark the silver jubilee of King George V in May 1935. The platforms at Prestatyn were timber built at this time and what looks like rather crude, hand-painted platform numbers have been applied to the ends of their wooden canopies.

As well as having the world's first named train, another innovation associated with the railway from Chester to Holyhead was that it was the location of the world's first water troughs. A steam locomotive can usually carry enough coal to enable it to travel a long distance, but having enough water for a long journey is a very different matter. In an effort to speed up the *Irish Mail* in 1860, the LNWR laid down the world's first water troughs at Mochdre near Conwy. These were literally wooden troughs laid between the rails on a level stretch of line which were then filled with water. A scoop was fitted to the tender of a locomotive which was lowered into the trough as it sped over it, forcing 100s of gallons of water into the tender. Water troughs enabled locomotives to travel long distances without having to stop to replenish their tenders

and soon became a feature of many British main lines with high volumes of traffic. There were several sets on the Chester to Holyhead line. The ones seen here near Prestatyn were 510 yards long, installed in 1885 and taken out of service in 1965. Ex-LMS rebuilt Royal Scot class 4-6-0 No 46136 *The Border Regiment* is on an Up parcels train on 22nd August 1958. To the left of the locomotive the start of the water troughs on the Down line can be seen.

RHYL

About four miles to the west of
Prestatyn was another of the great
resort towns created by this railway,
Rhyl. The extent and complexity of
the track layout at the east end of the
station is testament to the amount of
holiday traffic it had to deal with in its
heyday. Ex-LMS Black Five 4-6-0 No
45188 approaches Rhyl in July 1962
with a Down excursion heading for yet
another of those north Wales resorts,
Llandudno. The large structures to the
right of the train were carriage sheds.
Rhyl also had an engine shed which
had the code 7D in BR days.

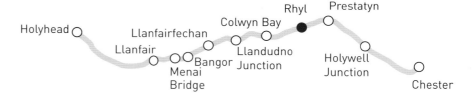

On 23rd August 1958, ex-LMS Royal Scot class 4-6-0 No 46141 *The North Staffordshire* Regiment pauses at Rhyl station with an express passenger train. The two small boys gazing in awe at the locomotive were almost certainly train spotters. This was an enormously popular hobby for small boys and many who were not so small at this time. If this was their first Royal Scot then they had another 70 to spot before they could 'cop' the whole class!

The line continued to hug the coast as it carried on westwards though Abergele & Pensarn station towards Colwyn Bay. On 3rd June 1963 ex-LMS Black Five 4-6-0 No 44760 has left Colwyn Bay and is seen here heading an express passenger train eastwards towards the site of Old Colwyn station, which closed in 1952. No 44760, built at Crewe in 1947 and withdrawn in October 1967, was one of a small batch of Black Fives experimentally fitted with Timken roller bearings rather than conventional axle boxes.

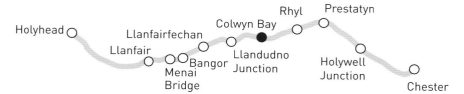

COLWYN BAY

Holyhead · Llanfairfechan · Llanfair · Bangor · Menai Bridge · Colwyn Bay · Llandudno Junction · Rhyl · Prestatyn · Holywell Junction · Chester

This striking portrait of the Up *Irish Mail* passing Colwyn Bay is from the early LMS era in the 1920s, when ex-LNWR locomotives were still dominant on the line. The leading or pilot engine is an ex-LNWR Prince of Wales class 4-6-0 No 5546 *Middlesex*, whilst the train engine is ex-LNWR Claughton class 4-6-0 No 5903 *Duke of Sutherland*. The locomotive department of the LMS in the 1920s was dominated by engineers from another of the new company's constituents, the Midland Railway, who seemed to take a dim view of the engines that had been built by their former great rival, the LNWR. The result was that many LNWR locomotives were withdrawn after relatively short careers.

This view of a service leaving Colwyn Bay and heading west towards Llandudno Junction is undated, but judging from the six-wheeled coaches which make up the train, it is probably from the first decade of the last century. The LNWR was a very early advocate of standardisation. Between 1858 and 1872 Crewe works turned out 943 of its DX class 0-6-0s, and the locomotive seen here is from another very numerous late nineteenth century type of 0-6-0, of which 310 were built between 1880 and 1902. Officially they were called 18 inch goods engines but were commonly known by their nickname, Cauliflowers.

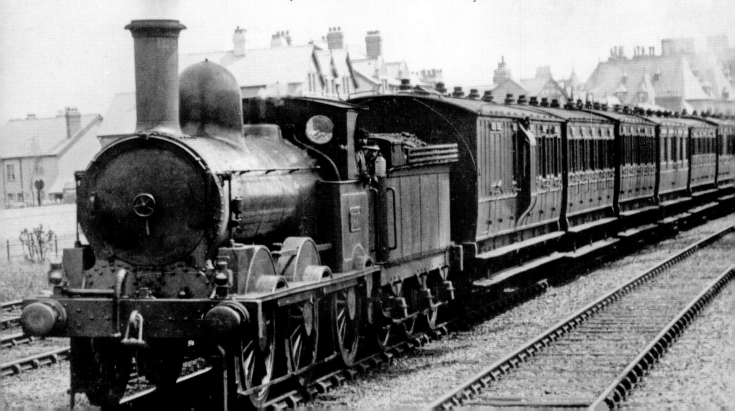

The two tracks through Colwyn Bay broadened out to four again on the section to Llandudno Junction. In August 1964 another of the ubiquitous ex-LMS Black Five 4-6-0s No 44684 built at Crewe in 1945 is heading towards Colwyn Bay on a stopping train on the Up slow line.

Approaching Llandudno Junction on the Down fast line is an example of one of the small class of 40 2-6-0s which constituted Sir William Stanier's first design for the LMS following his appointment as Chief Mechanical Engineer in 1932. The locomotive seen here is No.42966, built at Crewe in 1933. Only one member of this class was preserved, No.42968, which is based at Bridgnorth on the Severn Valley Railway in Shropshire.

One traffic flow that was very important to this line was the transport of live cattle from Ireland, which had been brought over on the steamers arriving at Holyhead. On the other side of the Irish Sea this also kept many Irish railways very busy, as long trains of cattle wagons made their way to Dublin and other ports on the east coast from fairs in the south and west of the country. Cattle wagons, unlike most goods wagons in use during the age of steam, usually had continuous brakes operated from the locomotive, similar to those on passenger trains. This enabled them to travel faster than normal goods trains which was essential to enable the animals to get to their destinations as quickly as possible and without undue delay or distress, even if this was also hastening their progress to the abattoir in many cases. Here, an unidentified ex-LMS Black Five hauls a long cattle train from Holyhead away from Llandudno Junction on the Up fast line. The River Conwy can be glimpsed in the distance beyond the trees.

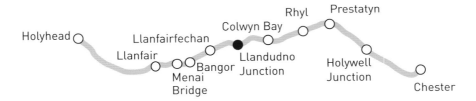

LLANDUDNO JUNCTION

Holyhead ○ — Llanfair ○○ ● Menai Bridge / Bangor — Llanfairfechan ○ — Llandudno Junction ● — Colwyn Bay ○ — Rhyl ○ — Prestatyn ○ — Holywell Junction ○ — Chester ○

The main reason for the demise of so many former LNWR engines in the years after grouping was the influx of those built by the LMS to Midland Railway designs such as No 41120, seen here on a local train at Llandudno Junction. This was constructed at the former Lancashire & Yorkshire Railway works at Horwich in 1925, based on a MR design dating back to 1902. This was a 'compound' locomotive which used the steam produced by the boiler twice, first in a high pressure cylinder from whence it was in effect recycled

and used again in low pressure cylinders, the ones on the outside. This early 1950s view shows the locomotive with its new BR number on its smokebox, though the initials LMS can still be seen on her tender. Llandudno Junction was a big station, with six through lines and two bay platforms at either end. The two branch lines which met the Coast Line here, those to Llandudno and Blaenau Festiniog, are still open, allowing Llandudno Junction to retain its function as an important interchange.

Immediately after leaving Llandudno Junction, the line crossed the estuary of the Conwy River on the first of Stephenson's tubular bridges and skirted the walls of Conwy's thirteenth century castle. The towers at the ends of the bridge were castellated in an attempt to blend in with the adjacent castle. In this 1935 view, LMS Royal Scot class 4-6-0 No 6124 *London Scottish*, in its original condition in which it ran between 1927 and its rebuilding in 1948, is passing through Conwy station on the Up *Irish Mail*. Conwy station was closed in 1966 but reopened in 1987.

It is unimaginable that planning permission would be given today for a railway to run as close to such an important heritage site as Conwy Castle. The decision to cross the river near the castle also meant that the station and its goods yard had to be squeezed into a very confined space, with the station built on a curve. On 17th August 1958, a stopping train for Holyhead is leaving Conwy hauled by BR Standard class 5 4-6-0 No 73071. Introduced in 1951 and best described as a BR version of the LMS Black Fives, a total of 172 of these locomotives were built.

Increasing traffic volumes throughout the nineteenth century had led to most of the line between Chester and Llandudno Junction being quadrupled by the time of the Great War, however, west of the Llandudno Junction double track sufficed. A long goods train from Holyhead approaches Conwy on 9th May 1963, hauled by ex-LMS Black Five 4-6-0 No 45043.

Having tunneled through the headland at Penmaenbach and still skirting the coast, the line reached Penmaenmawr. Quarries on the hill beside the station provided a useful supply of ballast for the railway over the years. On 14th August 1964, a Holyhead to Crewe parcels train heads east from Penmaenmawr, hauled by ex-LMS Coronation Pacific 4-6-2 No 46240 *City of Coventry*. The fact that such a locomotive was being used on a parcels train was a sign of the times. The Coronation Pacifics had been the LMS' most powerful main line express locomotives when introduced in 1937. Designed to haul the heaviest and fastest expresses on the West Coast Main Line between London Euston and Glasgow Central, by this time they were being displaced from those duties by diesel and electric traction and were seen increasingly on more humble duties such as this.

LLANFAIRFECHAN

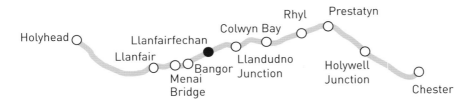

Holyhead ○

Llanfairfechan

Llanfair ○

Menai
Bridge ○

Bangor ●

Colwyn Bay ○

Llandudno
Junction ○

Rhyl ○

Prestatyn ○

Holywell
Junction ○

Chester ○

A few miles west of Penmaenmawr
was the next station, Llanfairfechan.
Approaching with a 4-coach local
passenger train is ex-LMS Black Five
No 45382. The scene here is much
changed since this 1950s view, as the
A55 dual carriageway has now been
squeezed in between the railway and
the town.

The narrow gauge Penrhyn Railway dated back to the early nineteenth century and was used to bring slate from quarries at Bethesda down to the coast at Port Penrhyn for shipment. When the C&H opened a short branch was built to Port Penrhyn to enable some of this slate traffic to go by rail. The junction for this line was about a mile east of Bangor. Up to 1954 there had been a signalbox here called Penrhyn Siding to control the junction, but this was replaced by a ground frame controlled by the nearby Bethesda Junction box, which was only about 500 yards to the west where the branch line to Bethesda diverged. Passing the line leading to Port Penrhyn is an Up goods hauled by Black Five No 45070.

BANGOR

Holyhead ○
Llanfairfechan
Llanfair ○
Menai Bridge
Bangor ●
Colwyn Bay ○
Llandudno Junction ○
Rhyl ○
Prestatyn ○
Holywell Junction ○
Chester ○

Bangor was another large and impressive station on this line. Some 60 miles from Chester, it was the original terminus of the C&H in 1848 while the bridge over the Menai Straits and the rest of the line to Holyhead was being constructed. The station site was hemmed in by tunnels on the approach from both directions, yet there was still room for two long island platforms and an engine shed.

The whole area was controlled by two large LNWR signal boxes at either end of the station, one of which is seen to the right of the picture. On the 11th June 1949, rebuilt ex-LMS Royal Scot class 4-6-0 No 46166 *London Rifle Brigade* is not stopping here as she takes the Up through road with the *Irish Mail*.

The platforms at Bangor were linked by the impressive covered footbridge seen behind Black Five No 44740 on a passenger train to Holyhead. This locomotive was one of a handful built in 1948 that were equipped with Caprotti valve gear. This was the invention of an Italian engineer, Arturo Caprotti, that used camshafts and poppet valves rather than conventional piston valves to transmit steam to the cylinders and allow it to be exhausted through the chimney. These locomotives had a very distinctive appearance with large steam pipes leading to their cylinders.

As well as the expresses to and from London and Manchester, slow passenger trains calling at intermediate stations and through freights, most of the stations along the line had their own goods yards which were served daily by pick up goods trains which called to set down or collect wagons. On 27th May 1947, one such working is seen shunting in the yard at Menai Bridge, west of Bangor, the last station before the line crossed over the Straits and into Anglesey. The loco is ex-LNWR Webb designed 2-4-2 tank No 6710, one of a class of 160 built at Crewe in the 1890s.

The Up *Irish Mail* sweeps around the curve leading off the Britannia Bridge in this classic view from the LNWR era. The leading engine is LNWR Precursor class 4-4-0 No 675 *Adjutant* and the train engine is unnamed LNWR Prince of Wales class 4-6-0 No 2073. The height of the towers bearing the original cast iron tubes is apparent, as are the pair of ornamental sculptures of lions beside the tracks. There was another pair on the approach to the other side of the bridge.

LLANFAIR

The first station in Anglesey was Llanfair, which opened on 1st August 1848 as a temporary terminus for trains from Holyhead, pending the completion of the Britannia Bridge. The village it served was known as Llanfair or Llanfairpwllgwyngyll, but it seems that sometime in the 1860s it was decided, as some sort of publicity stunt, to confer on the station the longest name in Britain. This was done by adding descriptions of nearby features such as ogof goch (red cave) to the village's name. The LMS was still clearly milking this for all it could in this late 1920s publicity shot, which

shows the then new Royal Scot class No 6117 *Welsh Guardsman* arriving at the station with the nameboard and a lady in Welsh costume emphasising the message. The station closed in 1966, but following the fire which closed the Britannia bridge in 1970 it was reopened and reprised its 1840s role as a temporary terminus for trains from Holyhead. The temporary station closed in 1972 but was rebuilt and re-opened in 1973. Now known as Llanfairpwll, the revived station has a good service of trains in both directions.

Holyhead •   Llanfairfechan   Colwyn Bay   Rhyl   Prestatyn

Llanfair   Llandudno   Holywell

Bangor   Junction   Junction

Menai   Chester

Bridge

The station at Holyhead today dates from the 1860s, when it was rebuilt by the LNWR. It was constructed on a 'V' shape, serving both sides of the inner harbour and allowing quick and easy access between trains and steamers. A hotel was situated in the centre of that 'V'. Ferries today use the outer harbour so passengers arriving by rail have to be bussed to the ships but at least it is still rail connected and as

such continues to provide the service for which it was built. In August 1951, rebuilt Royal Scot class 4-6-0 No 46159 *Lancashire Fusilier* is ready to leave the station with an express to Euston.

It seems an appropriate way to end this short survey of the Chester to Holyhead railway with this view of the *Irish Mail*, the world's first named train still going strong in August 1951, over 100 years since it first appeared in the timetables. The locomotive blasting away from Holyhead is Royal Scot class 4-6-0 No 46159 *The Royal Air Force* at the start of the train's long journey to Euston, over 260 miles away.

CREDITS

Lost Lines of Wales – Chester to Holyhead
Published in Great Britain in 2017
by Graffeg Limited

Written by Tom Ferris copyright © 2017.
Designed and produced by Graffeg
Limited copyright © 2017

Graffeg Limited, 24 Stradey Park
Business Centre, Mwrwg Road,
Llangennech, Llanelli, Carmarthenshire
SA14 8YP Wales UK Tel 01554 824000
www.graffeg.com

Tom Ferris is hereby identified as the
author of this work in accordance with
section 77 of the Copyrights, Designs and
Patents Act 1988.

A CIP Catalogue record for this book is
available from the British Library.

ISBN 9781912050697

1 2 3 4 5 6 7 8 9

Photo credits
© Ronnie Simpson, Online Transport
Archive: page 14.
© Kidderminster Railway Museum: pages
16, 18, 22, 23, 24, 26, 29, 30, 31, 33, 34, 36,
37, 40, 43, 44, 45, 46, 49, 51, 56.
© W. A. Camwell/SLS Collection:
pages 19, 20, 21, 54.
© R F Roberts SLS collection: pages
61, 63.
© John Worley, Online Transport Archive:
page 35.
© SLS Collection: page 58.
© Peter N Wilson, Online Transport
Archive: pages 12, 38, 52.

Titles in the Lost Lines of Wales series:

Cambrian Coast Line
ISBN 9781909823204

Aberystwyth to Carmarthen
ISBN 9781909823198

Brecon to Newport
ISBN 9781909823181

Ruabon to Barmouth
ISBN 9781909823174

Chester to Holyhead
ISBN 9781912050697

Shrewsbury to Aberystwyth
ISBN 9781912050680

The Mid Wales Line
ISBN 9781912050673

Vale of Neath
ISBN 9781912050666